LIVING LIFE WELL

By
Dr. James R. Love, Sr.

Copyright © 2014 by Dr. James R. Love, Sr.

Living Life Well
by Dr. James R. Love, Sr.

Printed in the United States of America

ISBN 9781628717747

All rights reserved solely by the author. The author guarantees all contents are original and do not infringe upon the legal rights of any other person or work. No part of this book may be reproduced in any form without the permission of the author. The views expressed in this book are not necessarily those of the publisher.

Unless otherwise indicated, Bible quotations are taken from the New King James Version. Copyright © 1982 by Thomas Nelson, Inc., Publishers. Other versions used include: The New Testament in Modern English, copyright © 1959 by MacMillan Company; THE MESSAGE, copyright © 2002 by Eugene H. Peterson; the New Living Translation copyright © 2007 by Tyndale House Foundation, and the Common English Bible, copyright © 2011.

www.xulonpress.com

I dedicate this book to my mother Vernell Bowie
and Elder Mary Lee Meares
"To live is what you are alive to!"
Maltbie Babcock

Acknowledgements

I give a profound thank you to Sister Cynthia Pillow for the exceptional effort in making this book a reality: Sister Pillow, you are simply the best!

A special word of thanks goes to Elder LaDorothy Pittman for typing the early rough draft of this book.

And many thanks to Reverend, Doctor Francina Kerr for her hard work in bringing this book into fruition

Finally, to my wife of over thirty years, who remain my chief critic and ardent supporter.

Table of Contents

Introduction xi
Preface: Living Life Well xvii
1. Live to Worship God 27
2. Live in the Fear of God 33
3. Live in Your Purpose with Passion 39
4. Live Within Satisfying Relationships 45
5. Live in the Power of Forgiveness 53
6. Live Embracing Brokenness 59
7. Live Life With Joy/Laughter 67
8. Live By Not Thinking Like
   The World 73
9. Live By Developing an
   Eternal Perspective 79
10. Live By The Motto: Don't Worry-
    Talk to God 83
11. Lessons Learned Over A Lifetime 89
Endnotes. 95

Introduction

I experienced a myocardial infarction ...a heart attack in September 1996 while preaching at Evangel Church, Upper Marlboro, MD. To learn about my experience, read the fine book by reporter, Bruce Johnson [the name of the book is "Heart to Heart", published by iUniverse, 2009]. After that episode, my doctor, Joseph Robinson, had been monitoring my cardiac health each year. For example, I would have an annual nuclear stress test that provided the doctor with detailed three-dimensional pictures of my inner heart chambers. Since I had been active in exercising, walking 4-5 miles every other day, and eating healthier, I thought my health trajectory was moving in a sound direction. However, there was a dark cloud forming which would turn me upside down.

I suppose this all started in 2008 when Dr. Robinson mentioned that he was a little concerned that the stress test was showing a gradual increase of plaque building up around the inner chambers of my heart. He said, "Doc, I want to run a few tests which will give a clearer picture of what's going on with your heart. I have some suspicions, but I want to be sure." So, on December 5, 2011, I went to the Washington Hospital Center to have a CAT scan of my heart. The doctor who administered the test informed me that because of my creatinine level (this tells the doctor the functioning of the kidneys) he could not do the full test but he could only do a scan of my chest. The test results revealed there was a tremendous amount of calcium building up around my heart. My calcium score was very high–in the 99th percentile!

With this information, Dr. Robinson recommended I go through a heart catheterization test...this is where they run a catheter through your veins to determine if there is any blockage. This test revealed that I had blockage in two places around the heart... the doctor who administered the test showed my wife the pictures!

I am pursuing this course, and I beg your indulgence, because it will provide you some insight into my psyche and into what motivated me to write this book. After all these tests, Dr. Robinson called me and I could tell from his tone that he regretted the news he was about to share. He said, "Doc, I am sorry to inform you that bypass surgery will be necessary, I am so sorry." I said, "Are you talking about open heart surgery?" He said, "Yes sir". While I was still at the hospital, Dr. Robert Lowery, an associate of Dr. Robinson, stepped into my room and concurred with Dr. Robinson's conclusion. I recall him saying I would be able to go a while without this procedure;

Introduction

however, based upon the test, it was just a matter of time before I would have another heart episode. I was inclined to delay until after Christmas but my wife of 31 years said that I should not delay; so I did what any well-trained husband would do, and said, "Let's do as she said!"

Dr. Lowery performed the triple bypass procedure, and while I in the recovery room, he informed me that the surgery was a success. I thanked him, but I really was thankful to the Lord.

For the next three days, while in recovery, I thought about how much I really wanted to go home before Christmas. All I could think about in the moments immediately after the surgery was, "Lord, I don't want to spend Christmas in the hospital!" Thank God, I was released on Christmas Eve. While I was in the hospital, I started thinking more seriously about my health; my future; the future of my wife and kids, and about Love The Gospel Church, where I serve as senior pastor. I strongly sensed that the Lord, in His grace, was giving me another chance. I must confess that I have been trying to write this book for over two years! I have been plagued by my own lack of focus and my dilatory attitude about this project...writing is really hard! However, since my recovery, I feel a new sense of vim and vivaciousness, as well as a new sense of purpose.

All that I have just said is to explain why I have undertaken this effort; however, a few nettlesome questions kept preoccupying my mind. First, what did Jesus mean by the statement in John 10:10, "The thief does not come except to steal, and to kill, and to destroy. I have come that they may have life, and that they may have it more abundantly." So, what is this abundant life He spoke about? How do I access it? Second, a student in my Introduction to Philosophy class at Prince George's Community College asked, "Professor Love, if there is so much pain, suffering, and injustice in the world, then just what is the meaning of life at all? We are all going to die anyway?" The statement, "what is the meaning", just stuck in my mind for some reason. Now, I have been asked this question a million times and have in fact asked it myself! As I lay in the hospital with IVs stuck in my arms, sore and exhausted, I echoed the question repeatedly in my mind: "What does it all mean?"

I am convinced that God has given humankind life and with it He has also given us an

inherent sense of meaning. Why else would we keep asking the question? I am reminded of the word of my favorite philosopher St. Augustine who said, "Our hearts are restless, until it finds rest in You." So, I thought that surely the author of life and death has a design for each of us and that in the Bible, He has made known that design. Thus, our life is best spent living an intentional lifestyle as Jesus did: a lifestyle, which was not independent of God, but dependent upon His will.

The ancient Greek philosophers were very interested in the question of how to live the best life. From Plato to Aristotle to Epicurus to Stoics, all asked how does one experience what they called "eudaimonia" which means human flourishing or happiness? Their answers range from pleasure, to emotional detachment, to practicing the cardinal virtues. However, for me, the real answer can only come from the creator of life...the living God, which has fundamentally been revealed in the Bible.

Dr. James R. Love, Sr.
January 2012

PREFACE
"LIVING LIFE WELL"
James 5: 3-6; John 11:25 (NKJV)

—⚞—

The preacher said it well when he said, "Life is hard!" Everyone is seeking some form of happiness and self-fulfillment, but how do you achieve it? Here is where the question of one's purpose comes into the mind of many people. It seems to me that the quintessential questions since time began are:

1. How do you live the best life? This is a question, which occupied the thoughts of some of the great minds of the ancient philosophers from Plato to Aristotle, to the insightful Stoic philosopher, Epictetus, who saw living life well as synonymous with the virtuous life.
2. What is my purpose? This is a question, which everyone at some point in life will ask. It was Viktor Frankl, who survived a Nazi concentration camp in WWII, who wrote in

his famous book, *Man's Search for Meaning* that "man's search for meaning" is the primary motivation in his life"[1]…

3. Why is life so hard? I often wonder why things in life seem so hard; like writing this book, for example. I have been working on this for two years, at least. Why is writing or achieving any pre-determined goal so challenging? I now agree with cynical Job when he said, "Man who is born of woman is of few days and full of trouble" (Job 14:1).

Moreover, along this line of thought, the immensely popular book by Rick Warren, *The Purpose Driven Life*[2], asked the question, "What drives your life?" I believe we are driven or perhaps better said motivated by many things…fame, fortune, etc. , However, Warren identifies five qualities that drive people.

1. Many people are driven by guilt. As a pastor, I have counseled many people who are driven, often manipulated, by the guilt of poor past choices, such as sexual immorality.
2. Many people are driven by resentment and anger. I have had husbands walk out of a counseling session, calling me everything but a child of God, because the counsel I gave confronted an area of sin in their lives.
3. Many people are driven by fear. There is certainly no doubt that fear in its various forms– from fear of heights, to fear of closed-in

spaces, to fear of speaking in front of a crowd–controls many lives. Some years ago, I preached a message called, "What Would I Achieve if I Wasn't Afraid?" Many people came up to me afterwards and confessed that I had addressed a fear issue within their lives.

4. Many people are driven by materialism. There is no doubt in my mind that this age is certainly characterized by conspicuous consumption. At the time of this writing, Apple has introduced the iPhone 5. It seemed like a year or two prior, they just introduced the iPhone4! Nevertheless, millions of people will buy the iPhone5 even though, to my untrained eyes, there is not much difference between them!

5. Many people are driven by the need for approval. I believe far too many people suffer from poor self-image and practice negative self-talk and they are often motivated to seek the praise or approval of others. For example, a teenage girl seeking the approval of a non-communicative father may seek such affirmation from boys through her provocative dress.

Regardless of what drives your life, the Bible is very clear that one day you will have to give an account to God for the life you were given. In short, the question is, "Did you live life well?" In Matthew 12:36, Jesus said, "...for every idle word men may speak, they will give account of it in the Day of

Judgment." Also, in Revelation 20:11-13, the idea is clearly presented by the image of the Great White Throne Judgment and the opening of the books. The basic operating principles upon which this book is written are:

1. To answer the question: What is the abundant life of which Jesus spoke of in John 10:10, "I came that you might have life and that more abundantly."
2. To prove that the best life is lived well in complete dependence upon Jesus Christ.
3. To show that the life of Jesus Christ is the quintessential example of a life lived well.

The source of this quote is unknown but saintly Mother Theresa of Calcutta, India once said...

"Life is an opportunity – benefit from it.
Life is a beauty – admire it.
Life is a dream – realize it.
Life is a challenge – meet it.
Life is a duty – complete it.
Life is a game – play it.
Life is a promise – fulfill it.
Life is sorrow – overcome it.
Life is a song – sing it.
Life is a struggle – accept it.
Life is a tragedy – confront it.
Life is an adventure – dare it.
Life is luck – make it.
Life is life – fight for it!"[3]

I believe that living well in this life is a precursor to living eternally in the next life. It was at the tomb of Lazarus that Jesus said something that is most profound regarding the continuity of life even after death. In John 11:25-26, in response to Martha's query, Jesus said, "I am the resurrection and the life. He that believeth in me, though he were dead, yet shall he live: and whosoever liveth and believeth in me shall never die. Believeth thou this?" The meaning is clear that Jesus has the power through His spoken words to speak life to situations where death has occurred.

Earlier we spoke about the question on the meaning and purpose of life. There is no doubt that this is one of the seminal questions in human history. There have been many responses to this question:

- Charles Darwin said that we accidentally evolved from apes and so life has no real meaning because human life is a cosmic accident.
- Frank Kafka, a 1930's French writer said that life is meaningless and absurd.
- William Shakespeare said, "Life's but a walking shadow, a poor player. That struts and frets his hour upon the stage. And then is heard no more."
- Jean-Paul Sartre, the existentialist French writer of the 1930's said, "Existence precedes essence." You are whatever you choose.

- St Augustine said that life is a unique gift from God…"our hearts are restless until it finds rest in You, O Lord."

What do I mean by Living Life Well? We have to make a distinction between physical life or biology and spiritual life or according to the Greek language zoë. Our physical bodies are composed of material matter, bones, tissues, muscles, etc. As long as we take good care of our physical bodies, we will live and thrive. However, the Christian knows that life is more than just physical or biological. There is another aspect of life, which is spiritual or zoë. The spiritual dimension is just as real, though it is non-physical. For example, I have a cell phone and though I don't see the signal, which allows me to talk to people all around the nation, the signal is invisible but it is nonetheless very real. So it is with spiritual realities. They are not material or physical, but they do exhibit tangible qualities. I believe this is what Jesus had in mine in John 10:10.

I think too many Christians live life only on a physical level, neglecting God. Dr. Tony Evans was correct when he wrote, "every physical reality is first directed by a corresponding spiritual reality."[4] God intended for us to live life directed by the Holy Spirit who lives within us and gives meaning and purpose.

The Bible is clear that God intends for humanity to live in a state of intimate relationship with Him. Perhaps the best news that Christianity offers to a lost world is the news that God isn't mad at us, but that He really desires a relationship with us. For example, III

John 2 says, "Beloved, I pray that you may prosper in all things and be in health, just as your soul prospers." And Job 10:12 states, "You have granted me life and favor and Your care has preserved my spirit." The psalmist writes in Psalms 119:50,"For Your word has given me life." Again, Galatians 2:20 says, "I have been crucified with Christ; it is no longer I who live, but Christ lives in me; and the life which I now live in the flesh I live by faith in the Son of God, who loved me and gave Himself for me."

God will not impose this life upon you; you must make a decision. Look at the decision God placed before Israel in Deuteronomy 30:15-20 "...life and good, death and evil?" In addition, The Westminster Catechism states, "What is the chief end of man? To glorify God and enjoy Him forever." In other words, the nation of Israel had to choose.

Rick Warren in his great book, *The Purpose Driven Life,* was right when he wrote,

- "Life is a test, meaning that there will be tribulations.
- Life is trust, meaning God who owns everything has given us a stewardship.
- Life is a temporary assignment, meaning that compared to eternity, life is temporary."[5]

Finally, if life is supposed to be so good, what happened to mess things up? Please bear with me as I give a biblical response to this query. What happened can be summed in what theologians call "The Fall".

In Genesis 1:26-28, God created our first parents, Adam and Eve, for the express purpose of cultivating a personal relationship with them. The imagery of God meeting with them in the "cool of the day" is HEBREWISM…a way of saying they had a personal, intimate relationship. Now with this authentic relationship, God placed Adam and Eve in a garden and gave them a choice. There were two trees within this garden, the tree of life, and the tree of the knowledge of good and evil. Unfortunately, Adam and Eve chose to disobey God by partaking from the tree of the knowledge of good and evil (Genesis 3:6-8). Their decision had catastrophic consequences for the cosmos and for the future of humankind (Romans 5:12 -21). In their choosing to eat of the tree of the knowledge of good and evil, there were four unintended consequences:

- Shame–they were naked and a sense of shame overwhelmed them;
- Guilt–they experienced a sense of guilt; their conscious informed them that they had done something horribly wrong;
- Estrangement–they experienced a strong sense of shifting blame to the other for the situation, and
- Despair–they experienced an overwhelming sense of hopelessness.

Therefore, what happened is best summed up by the word SIN, which is a missing of the mark, straying from God's intended purpose. It is sin that caused a Holy God to turn away from us in judgment, and because of our choices to do it our way, I believe, it is the reason why the world is in the predicament it is in today! One final note, because humankind has to deal with the troubling vicissitudes of life, today, like never before, there is the overwhelming emotions of hopelessness, despair, fear, and forbearing pessimism about the future.

But, thanks be to God the Bible says, "Where sin abound, grace did much more abound," (Romans 5:20). Edward Mote, the hymn writer said it well, "my hope is built on nothing less than Jesus' blood and righteousness; I dare not trust the sweetest frame, but wholly lean on Jesus' name. On Christ the solid rock I stand, all other ground is sinking sand." [6] I believe if you and I intend to live well, then we need to obtain a new vision of the splendor of Jesus; there aren't enough superlatives to describe Him:

You see Jesus came to give us new life...

You see Jesus came to show us how to live life...

You see Jesus is our model for living life as God originally intended for it to be lived...

You see Jesus came to forgive us of our sin...

You see Jesus came to show us the awesome love of the Father...

You see Jesus has done for us what we could not do for ourselves...

Finally, the rest of this book will focus upon the following topics, as I firmly believe they provide for you the steps to take in the process of Living Life Well:

1. Live to Worship God–you and I were created to worship the living God.
2. Live in the Fear of God–you must live out what it means to reverence the living God.
3. Live in Your Purpose with Passion–you will never be satisfied until you find your purpose and your passion in life.
4. Live Within Satisfying Relationships–you are designed for satisfying relationships.
5. Live in the Power of Forgiveness–you will be hurt or wounded, but forgiveness is really in your best interest.
6. Live Embracing Brokenness–you must understand that our world is broken, particularly as it relates to human relationships.
7. Live Life With Joy/Laughter–you must learn to laugh and not take life so seriously.
8. Live by Not Thinking like Worldly People–you must recognize that the devil desires to shape the way you think, he wants to assault your mind.
9. Live By Developing An Eternal Perspective–you must adopt an eternal perspective and reject the temporary perspective of this world.
10. Live By The Motto: Don't Worry Talk to God–you must embrace the mindset that worry is contrary to the purposes of God in your life.
11. Lessons Learned Over a Lifetime–you must come to grips with the fact that life reflection is crucial.

CHAPTER 1

"LIVE TO WORSHIP GOD"

Luke 7:36 – 50 (NKJV)

Let's start our discussion about living life well with a very important concept: Live to Worship God! I firmly believe that at the core of our DNA, human beings are designed to worship the true and living God. Furthermore, I believe we are the most fulfilled when we realize and practice what we were designed for: Worship!

So what is worship and why is it so vital to living life well? Let's start with some basic definitions and biblical examples. The Hebrew word *SHACHAH* means to bow down or to prostrate oneself. A good example of this word in action is found in Genesis 18:2, which is the story when Abraham bows down to the three angelic visitors who came to judge Sodom and Gomorrah. Now, the Greek word *PROSKUNEO* has a slightly different connotation: It means to show reverence or to kiss. An example of this word in action is found in Luke 7:36-39, which is the story of this "sinful" woman who came one day to worship at the feet of Jesus.

What I take away from these two words for worship is this; that worship is not something we do as much as it is something we are! Therefore, worship is a lifestyle, a way of living out what God created us to be. You see, worship is an attitude of the heart, a reaching toward God, like a plant that is always reaching upward. Worship is the outpouring of our total self in thanksgiving, praise, adoration, and love to the living God who loves us.

True worship is discerning God's presence and responding to that presence with our whole being... mind, spirit, body. In his book, *Let Us Worship*, Judson Cornwall said, "worship speaks of God to God." [1]The reason why worship is so crucial to our living the best life is that worship allows us to gain access into the presence of God. You see, whereas, praise expresses thanks and appreciation to God for His wonderful acts, worship expresses simply motivation to be in His presence. David said in Psalms 16:11, "...In your presence is fullness of joy; at your right hand are pleasures forevermore." [Do you desire to sense the presence of God in your life?]

The biblical story cited above is about a nameless woman who crashed a party in order that she might worship at the feet of Jesus (v.36). A religious leader, a Pharisee, had asked Jesus to come over to his house for dinner. He wanted to have a theological conversation with Jesus. The Pharisees were a group of religious men who initially separated themselves from their fellow Jews in order to faithfully practice the law of Moses.

We know from what we observed in reading (vv 37-38), suddenly, this nameless woman appeared whom Luke calls a "sinner". Often she is confused with Mary Magdalene. This nameless woman starts to worship at the feet of Jesus by literally washing His feet with her tears! Moreover, she then took an alabaster flask filled with spikenard oil, very costly in that day, and poured it over the head of Jesus. Undoubtedly, the fragrance must have filled the room. In a symbolic way, the fragrance spoke of her deep worship of Jesus. This costly oil was typically used for the following purposes:

- in preparation of body for ceremonial burial
- in various Jewish religious feasts, or
- in purifying of the priest for their service to God

The depth of this woman's worship of Jesus certainly drew the ire of the Pharisee who observed her anoint Jesus' head with oil, kiss His feet, and dry His feet with her hair.

Probably, no longer able to contain himself (v.39), one of the Pharisees began to criticize Jesus and the sinful woman. Politely, though, he never spoke aloud what he was thinking to himself…No one was supposed to hear. You see, he thought to himself, "If this Jesus was a prophet of God, then He would discern what type of woman she is." This sinful woman, with her shady background, had done several things that were socially scandalous:

- she touched Jesus
- she let down her hair
- she expressed deep love and affection toward Jesus
- she poured (some considered it a waste) very costly oil on Jesus, and
- she kissed the feet of Jesus.

Aware of all the drama swirling around this incident (vv. 40-43), Jesus strangely responds by telling Simon a provocative story. The gist of the story is of two people who were in debt and how they both responded to the news that their debt had been cancelled. Now the one who had been forgiven the most debt obviously was much more appreciative than the one who had the smaller debt. Thus, the heart of the story is this question: Which one would express the most love toward the one who extended such a great kindness? Simon answered the question correctly, the one who was forgiven the larger sum of money.

I believe if you truly desired to live well, then just as the sinful woman manifested brokenness in her worship because she innately knew how much God had done for her, we must do likewise. How broken are you about sin in your life and does this motivate you to worship God in deep humility?

"Live to Worship God"

Jesus (vv 44-50) turns to the sinful woman and commends her for her service to Him. It appears as if the host did not perform the socially correct protocol of washing guest's feet and greeting them with a kiss on the cheek. I believe it was because of her brokenness and the deep humility with which she worshipped that Jesus extends to her undeserving grace. Observe what He does for the sinful woman:

- He extends to her forgiveness
- He commends her for exhibiting faith
- He grants to her much sought after inner peace, and
- He grants her deliverance from her tawdry past.

Finally, what was so unusual about this woman's worship that she was so blessed by Jesus?

The following are a few points I want you to take away from this chapter:

1. Brokenness – she knelt at the feet of Jesus. Worship requires brokenness as David said in Psalms 51:17, "The sacrifices of God are a broken spirit and a broken and contrite heart…"
2. Humility – she washed His feet with her tears and dried them with her hair…Worship requires humility.
3. Love – she passionately modeled her love for Jesus: Why such outpouring of emotion? Because if you only knew what she'd been

through all of her life, rejection, shame, guilt, and a sense of despair.

She poured all she had when she emptied her alabaster flask. Worship means giving all that you are and have to God. As I said earlier, the best life is one that is lived as worship unto God. I believe we are designed by God to worship and we are the most fulfilled doing what we were designed to do.

CHAPTER 2

"LIVE IN THE FEAR OF GOD"

Ecclesiastes 12:13-14 & Psalms 34:11-14 (NKJV)

Many Christians have become too familiar with the holy things of God. What I mean is too many Christians are so familiar with the sacraments that they have lost their power to create a sense of transcendence. As a result, they have lost the ability to awe inspire us. We have lost that sense of reverence. A study done several years ago by George Gallop showed 50 million Americans consider themselves born again but only 12% said that the demands of Jesus Christ had any effect upon their lifestyles. Therefore, 88% who claimed to be born again do not consider the demands of Jesus relevant to their lifestyle!

It shouldn't surprise anyone that today's culture has produced a spirit which lacks respect for any authority figure such as teachers, supervisors, pastors, etc. In this chapter, I want to discuss briefly living in the fear of the Lord as a crucial part of living well. What is very sad is that among Christians there exists a lack of the fear of the Lord. When I was a kid, it used to be commonplace that you would hear teachings about the fear of the Lord. Today this is not so common!

Why is there so little teaching done on the fear of the Lord?

1. We misunderstand what the term means and associate it with dread or natural fear
2. We misunderstand this with fear of heights, insects, claustrophobia, etc.
3. We misunderstand this with the fear of people (see Proverbs 29:25)

Bear in mind that one characteristic of the early Christians is that they understood the fear of the Lord. What should characterize a healthy Christian is the fear of the Lord. Acts 2:40-43 states, "...fear came upon every soul ", and Acts 5:11 states... "So great fear came upon all the church and upon all who heard these things."

The prophet Jeremiah gave a scathing indictment upon Israel because they had forgotten the fear of the Lord (Jeremiah 5:20-25). It is important that you understand this spiritual truth: Whatever you fear the most you will worship. And if you fear nothing, then you will worship yourself. Psalms 86:11 says, "Teach me your ways, O Lord; I will walk in your truth; Unite m heart to fear your name." So, what does the term "fear of the Lord" mean? Observe the following Scriptures:

> II Chronicles 19:7 – "Now therefore, let the fear of the Lord be upon you."
>
> Proverbs 15:16 – "Better is little with the fear of the Lord, than great treasure and trouble."

The Hebrew words morah means reverence, awe and pachad means startled, tremble. Therefore, the fear of the Lord isn't the kind of thing that means dread, like an abused wife might dread her husband coming home drunk.

According to W. E. Vines, *Expository Dictionary of New Testament Words*, "The fear of the Lord is a wholesome dread of displeasing Him."[1] This suggests that the person really does not want to disappoint God more than anything else.

My own definition is the following: The fear of the Lord is a vehement passion to please God more than anyone or anything; a reverence of His Holiness; a desire to please Him and walk in such a lifestyle that pleases Him. A good illustration of the fear of the Lord is found in the prophet Isaiah 66:1-2, the person who has a "contrite spirit, who trembles at His word."

In Ecclesiastes 12:13-14, Solomon is rather pessimistic about life; he sees it as vanity and fruitless. The only thing that makes sense to him is this: "Remember your creator while you are young because difficult days are ahead". Solomon believes that everyone must give an account for the life he has chosen to live to God. So he says in (vv 13-14) "Fear God and keep His commandments, this sums up all of life." I will return to this specific text in a later chapter where I will give some specific observations of Solomon's main point about the lessons he learned over a lifetime.

In Psalms 34: 11-14, David enunciates the specific components of understanding the fear of the Lord: Keep your tongue from evil, guard your mouth and be careful what you speak; lips from speaking deceit, be honest and truthful in your speaking; departs from evil and do good, watch your attitude and behavior, and, seek peace and pursue it, try to work with instead of against people.

Finally, I want to show you seven benefits the Scripture promises to those who learn how to fear the Lord:

1. The promise of wisdom ...(Proverbs 1:7; 15:33; Job 28:28; Psalm 111:10)
2. The promise of guidance, instruction, and prosperity... (Psalm 25:12-14)
3. The promise of spiritual cleansing... (Psalm 19:9)
4. The promise of long life... (Psalm 34:11-15)
5. The promise of deliverance from fear... (Proverbs 14:26-27)
6. The promise of abiding satisfaction and freedom...(Proverbs 19:23)

7. The promise of a secure future…(Proverbs 22:4; 23:17-18)

The real issue is whom do you desire to please–self, people, or God? Because whomever you please, is whom you fear. Whomever you fear is whom you will serve. Whomever you serve is whom you will worship. Whomever you worship is who you will become. Whom do you desire to please? And who are you becoming? Therefore, if you are going to live well, live in the fear of the Lord.

CHAPTER 3
"LIVE IN YOUR PURPOSE WITH PASSION"

Deuteronomy 29:29 (NKJV)

—⚋—

The quintessential question about our existence is: What is the purpose of life? It is this question, which has been asked since the dawn of history that has befuddled and perplexed human kind. The great Greek philosopher Aristotle asked what is the <u>telos</u> of man? He said it is to be happy and live a virtuous life. Also, the existentialist French writer of the 1940's, Albert Camus, said that life is absurd and meaningless. I agree with Dr. Myles Monroe who said, "The greatest tragedy in life is not death, but life without a reason. It is dangerous to live and not know why you were given life."[1] The deepest craving of the human spirit is to find a sense of significance and relevance. The search for relevance in life is the ultimate pursuit of humankind.

What I am discovering is that too few people actually stop to think about this question. We have moved from a thinking culture to a feeling culture. The culture doesn't promote critical thought but emotive reaction. People don't think about this because of the implications...maybe there is a God and we must give an account to Him.

Rick Warren said it well: "If you want to know why you were placed on this planet, you must begin with God. You were born by His purpose and for His purpose."[2] Here's my point: the purpose of a thing cannot be found within the thing itself. You must look outside the thing to discover the thing's purpose. Therefore, for a thing to look for a purpose within itself is irrational and foolish. Only the thing's designer can know what he had in mind when he created the thing. We waste so much time looking within for our purpose that we forgot we are creatures and God is the creator!

Thus, any hint of our purpose must come from God to us. Deuteronomy 29:29 says, "The secret things belong to the Lord our God, but those things which are revealed belong to us and to our children forever, that we may do all the words of this law." We are only responsible for light/knowledge, which God has revealed to us; we are not responsible for what has not been revealed to us.

Now, let's consider the word "purpose": Greek word *prosthesis* means a setting, to set before... Ephesians 1:11 "...predestined according to the purpose of Him who works all things according to the counsel of His will." Romans 8:28 "...all things work together for good to those who love God, to those who are called according to His purpose." Webster defines the word purpose as: the design, the objective for which something exists or the intent of something. Jeremiah 29:11 (NLT)..."For I know the plans I have for you, says the Lord. They are plans for good and not for disaster, to give you a future and a hope."

I believe with this knowledge, should we not we fall down on our knees and praise God for a purpose driven life? In his great book, *The Purpose Driven Life,* Pastor Rick Warren identified five particular purposes we all share:

1. "You were planned for God's pleasure," He takes great delight in you.
2. "You were formed for God's family," He has placed you within a specific family so that you would be nurtured.
3. "You were created to become like Christ," Your target is to evolve into someone, Jesus; people around you are not the standard, Jesus is.
4. "You were shaped for serving God," I believe it is in our DNA to serve that is the sense of helping, and working with others.
5. "You were made for a mission," [3] You won't live well until you figure out what your life's mission is.

Although I agree with all of the above; I believe there is a more basic understanding of purpose and it is transformation from within. When one talks about seeking one's purpose, typically, what we really mean is: give me a list of rules to follow or things to do. However, I am discovering that purpose has a lot more to do with me developing into a certain kind of person who is pleasing to God. Perhaps it is more salient to live a principle-centered life than a purpose-centered life. Maybe I am just using semantics, but I don't think so. Here is why. I believe "purpose" can have some degree of variation but principles don't vary, they are constant.

In Romans 12:1-2, we are called to lay our bodies upon the altar of sacrifice in service to God. The imagery is of an Old Testament animal sacrifice for atoning sin. The secret to a principle-centered life is, as J.B. Phillips, paraphrases these verses as follows: "Don't be conformed to the thinking of this world. Don't be squeezed into the mold of the world and its way of thinking."[4] You must be transformed by the renewing of your mind so let God remake your mind.

This addresses the question of purpose because it concerns the kind of person I am becoming, principle-centered, one who pleases God. Finally, in Thessalonians 4:1-7, Paul gives a general call to moral purity and purpose (The will of God…your sanctification). We must learn how to possess or control our fleshly desires according to God's standards.

This addresses the question of purpose because it concerns what God expects of me, moral purity. Living the best life is living with purpose and passion. What kind of person are you becoming? Are you walking out in your life God's holy purpose of sanctification?

As I said earlier, it was the question that perplexed me while I was recovering from bypass surgery. Does God have a purpose for my existence? God's purpose in my life is to take all my experiences, both good and bad, in order to produce in me the kind of person who would be pleasing to Him, who would be ready to live with Him throughout all eternity. Therefore, I will discover my purpose as I practice the godly principle of living life intentionally.

CHAPTER 4

"LIVE WITHIN SATISFYING RELATIONSHIPS"

Proverbs 17:17; 18:24 (NKJV)

Let's face it, we were created for satisfying and fulfilling relationships. We were not designed to live in isolation. That's why Genesis 2:18 says, "It is not good for man to be alone."

Back in the 1980s there was a popular sitcom called "Cheers." The theme song captures the mood of most people today:

> "Making your way in the world today
> Takes everything you've got.
> Taking a break from all your worries
> Sure would help a lot.
> Wouldn't you like to get away?
> All those nights when you got no lights,

> The check is in the mail.
> Sometimes you wanna go where
> Everybody knows your name and they're
> glad you came.
> You wanna be where you can see,
> Our troubles are all the same
> You wanna be where everybody knows
> your name."[1]

However, the state of relationships be they married, friendships, parental or with coworkers, is in trouble today. It seems to me, relationships are more difficult to develop and harder to maintain. There is no longer the commitment to work at establishing or maintaining relationships today. A "try and see" attitude exists. Yet, despite the fact that relationships are in trouble, we continue to strive to be in a relationship. How else would you explain the popularity of the on-line dating services such as eHarmony or match-date.com? The fundamental problem in relationships is that we are all at heart, selfish, self-centered, and self-sufficient. In addition, another thing that hinders our relationships is that our culture is "tuned in" technologically but is "tuned out" on connecting with someone else on a deep level. You see more people so enamored with their smart phones, iPads and the latest new technology than focused on relationships. We have more technology to communicate but, unlike prior generations, we connect less on a deeper level. To live well, one has to learn how to cultivate satisfying relationships. A little later in this chapter, I plan to show how this is done.

Both Proverbs 17:17 and 18:24 speaks of the relationship of friends. Keep in mind that there are different kinds of relationships:

- Husband – wife, this relationship is perhaps the most intimate…
- Parent – child, this relationship is very special; the miracle of childbirth is amazing…
- Teacher – student, this is a special bond that focuses upon instruction and education…
- Employer – employee, this is more professional and at times distant in terms of intimacy…
- Boyfriend – girlfriend, this is the starting point in terms of close intimacy outside of the husband – wife relationship.

Also, each of these relationships has a set of rules by which they operate in order to be successful. In other words, the nature or type of relationship will differ from one another. For example, you would not treat the husband/wife relationship the same way you would treat a parent/child relationship! Observe how the New Living Translation interprets these two texts: Proverbs 17:17 "A friend is always loyal and a brother is born to help in the time of need. Proverbs 18:24 states, "There are friends who destroy each other, but a real friend sticks closer than a brother."

How do we define friendship? As difficult as the definition may be, we must attempt to define it in order to talk about it. In a written survey of more than three hundred married and single men and women ranging in age from eighteen to eighty-two, each person was asked to write "a brief definition of a friend". Here are some characteristic replies:

- "Someone who you can bare your soul to and not be afraid it will get around. Someone who will tell you when your slip is showing. Someone who shares loving concern and tactful truth (woman, age thirty-one).
- "One who know you well and loves you anyway" (woman, age sixty-six).
- "Loyal in hard times, fun to be with, and have common interests" (man, age twenty-six)
- "A person who understands you and appreciates your views, loyal. A person who has quite a few common interests with you" (man, age fifty-five).
- "Someone who enjoys being around you, accepts you for who you are, and is faithful to you when the chips are down" (man, age twenty-four).
- "One who I can share my heart with no matter what is on it and still be accepted for who I am, and vice versa. One who I can be honest with for good or bad. One who I love being with and sharing things with. One who is a good listener" (woman, age twenty-nine).
- "A good friend is someone in whom you have unlimited trust; they will share with you deeply and honestly. The things shared between you go beyond opinions and observations" (woman, under thirty)

- "One who I can share my deepest thoughts, desires, and feelings with in confidence" (man age twenty-four)[2]

From a Christian perspective, a friend is a trusted confidant to whom I am mutually drawn as a companion and ally, whose love for me is not dependent on my performance, and whose influence draws me closer to God. If you are going to experience satisfying relationships, you must ask the question: Why is this person in my life? Observe this principle in 1 Samuel 20:17 which is the story of the deep relationship between David and Jonathan. Jonathan was the son of King Saul; however, he knew that David was anointed to be the next King of Israel. Yet he was loyal to David anyway. You will see this principle again in Acts 10:26-30…Barnabas developed a deep relationship with Paul who was a former persecutor of Christians. No one wanted anything to do with Paul!

The thing I want you to notice is that the success of each of these relationships was based upon adding value to the other person. There are too many toxic relationships were one person feels as if something has been taken from them. At this point, a word about what hinders relationships is in order. Check out the following:

1. One who can't keep confidences; no one wants to be friends with someone who can't maintain confidence.

2. Arrogance/pride, who wants to be friends with someone who belittles you, one who is primarily focused upon themselves.
3. Shy/withdrawn personality, this type of person never opens themselves to outside relationships.
4. Selfish, self-centered, self-sufficient, this is characteristic of most people, which is why it possesses such a challenge to relationships.
5. Angry spirit, now who wants to be around an erupting volcano?
6. Negative/critical spirit, who wants to be around someone who is always negative or critical
7. Bossiness/controlling, this is a major hindrance to relationships because it regards the other party as someone who needs to be managed or dominated.

Let's face it, we were created for satisfying and fulfilling relationships. In his must read book, *Connecting*, Dr. Larry Crabb says, "When two people connect, when their beings intersect…something is poured out of one and into the other that has the power to heal the soul of its deepest wounds and restore it to health."[3]

I need you and you need me! So, with this in mind let me give you my seven short principles to satisfying relationships:

1. Treat people as ends and not means to an end (Matthew 7:12)

"Live within Satisfying Relationships"

2. Be real…Be authentic (Colossians 2:22-23)
3. Don't be judgmental…Be more accepting (Matthew 7:1-6)
4. Learn how to speak the truth in love (Ephesians 4:15)
5. Enter into conflict very carefully (James 1:19-20)
6. Try to see people through the eyes of Jesus (Matthew 9:36)
7. Learn how to be a more loving person (1 Corinthians 13:1-3)

Relationships are critical to living the best life now. It's one thing to have a relationship with me; however, it's another thing to have a relationship with God through Jesus Christ. You see, I believe that ultimately, to live well one must commit to God through his Son Jesus Christ. A relationship with God is what puts all other relationships into perspective; it actually gives them meaning.

CHAPTER 5
"LIVE IN THE POWER OF FORGIVENESS"

Matthew 6:14-15 (NKJV)

On January 1984, Pope John Paul walked into a prison cell in Roman to meet Mehmet Ali Agca, the man who shot him. The Pope took the hand of the man who fired a bullet at his heart and forgave him! Forgiving is love's toughest assignment and its biggest risk. If you twist it into something it was never meant to be, it can make you a doormat or an insufferable manipulator.

Forgiveness is an unnatural thing to do. I want to talk with you about what forgiveness is not, what it is, and how to forgive totally. Because forgiveness is so difficult and so unnatural, Michele Nelson, in an article in "Christianity Today" called *"The Forgiveness Factor"*, spoke of degrees of forgiveness.

1. Detached forgiveness...There is a reduction of negative feelings toward the offender but no reconciliation.
2. Limited forgiveness...There is a reduction in negative feelings toward the offender and a partial restoration of the relationship.
3. Full forgiveness...There is no negative feelings toward the offender and the relationship is restored. [1]

What I want to show you is that forgiveness is ultimately a process:

- Stage one is the initial hurt, "Why did you hurt me?"
- Stage two is the initial hate, "I hate that you've caused me such pain and anxiety."
- Stage three is the initial healing, "It doesn't hurt as much, now"
- Stage four is the initial coming together, "I am willing to consider looking beyond my past hurt."

I believe R. T. Kendall is correct when he says in his book *Total Forgiveness*: "The person who gains the most from forgiveness is the person who does the forgiving." [2] However, before we can discuss what forgiveness means, we must first clarify what it does not mean:

1. Forgiveness is not a feeling; you won't feel like doing it.

2. Forgiveness is not pretending you were not hurt; honestly, the hurt might still be present.
3. Forgiveness is not condoning what the person did to you, you're not saying, "it's okay, that you hurt me". No.
4. Forgiveness is not trusting the offender, again, you are not saying, "I'm ok, but actually you are saying, I trust God."
5. Forgiveness is not relieving the person of responsibility, this is not make believe "The hurt really hurts and that is because of what you did".

Forgiveness is one of the most difficult decisions we will ever make in our lives. It is not easy nor is it simple. So why must I forgive? Jesus said in Matthew 6:14-15, "For if you forgive men their trespasses, your heavenly Father will also forgive you. But if you do not forgive men their trespasses, neither will your Father forgive your trespasses." In other words, we forgive because we have been forgiven. Matthew 5:23-24 says "When you come to the altar to bring a gift and you recall that your brother or sister has an offence against you, leave your gift and be reconciled to your brother or sister."

So what is forgiveness? I agree with R. T. Kendall when he said, "The ultimate proof of total forgiveness takes place when we sincerely petition the Father to let those who have hurt us off the hook – even if they have not hurt us, but also those close to us."[3] In essence, forgiveness means, to pardon; to give up all claims to punish or exact penalty; to give up all bitterness, resentment, and anger towards the offender. Therefore, the essence of the word is the undeserved release of an offender from the just punishment they deserve. Notice the following examples from the Scriptures:

- John 8:1-12…The woman caught in the act of adultery was forgiven by Jesus.
- Isaiah 1:18…"Come now, and let us reason together, says the Lord, though your sins are like scarlet, they shall be as white as snow; though they are red like crimson, they shall be as wool."
- Psalm 103:12…"As far as the east is from the west, so far has He removed our transgressions from us."
- Psalm 86:5…"For you, Lord, are good and ready to forgive, and abundant in mercy to all those who call upon you."
- Psalm 130:4…"But there is forgiveness with you, that you might be feared."

What I have discovered as a pastor and as a counselor about forgiveness is that it is very costly. The cost of forgiveness is worth it if you consider the alternative, which is vengeance. Forgiveness at least offers the chance of reconciliation and emotional peace. The person who benefits the most from forgiveness is the one doing the forgiving. Let me make three short points here:

1. We must learn how to forgive the offender; it's in your best interest.
2. We must learn how to forgive ourselves at times, if you have been a victim, sometimes you might feel it was your fault.
3. We must learn how to forgive God, by this we might think, "Why didn't God stop this?"

One day Peter asked Jesus this question: "Lord how often shall my brother sin against me, and I forgive him? Up to seven times?" Jesus' response was a shock, "I do not say to you, up to seven times, but up to seventy times seven"(Matthew 18:21-35). The point is we must cultivate an attitude of forgiveness that is ready whenever the occasion arises. Finally, what is the process which will help me to effectively learn how to forgive? R. T. Kendall said something that arrested my attention:

"You must totally forgive them. Until you totally forgive them you will be in chains. Release them, and you will be released."[4]

Again, the person who benefits the most from forgiveness is the one doing the forgiving. Finally, there are four principles about forgiveness that I have practiced over the years as a pastor:

1. Learn that the act of forgiveness is a choice which you must make as an act of faith
2. Learn that you must release the offender as an act of will and as an act of faith
3. Trust that God is the ultimate judge and He is just

- 1 Peter 3:21-23…Jesus gave it to God
- Romans 12:19-21… Don't avenge, give it to God
4. Move on…Train your thoughts not to dwell upon the past

Perhaps the best example of total forgiveness is none other than Jesus! While being crucified, He said, "Father forgive them for they don't know what they are doing" (Luke 23:24). So, I firmly believe if you really desire to live well, then you must robustly address the issue of unforgiveness in your life. Unforgiveness is like a poison in your spirit; it corrupts everything.

CHAPTER 6
"LIVE EMBRACING BROKENNESS"

Genesis 32:22-32 (NKJV)

After I experienced a heart attack about 10 years ago, I can recall lying in the ICU room thinking, "am I going to have to slow down my level of activities such as exercise, sex, travel?" In other words, was I destined to limp my way through the rest of my life? During those days of recovery, I had many questions but ultimately I was totally a broken man.

Have you ever experienced brokenness? Perhaps a trusted friend betrayed your trust. Perhaps it was the death of a spouse or a loved one. Perhaps it was a bad decision you made when you were younger and it continues to haunt you, even now. Perhaps you had a dream about what you would do or be but that dream has become a nightmare.

I have the opportunity to talk to broken people all the time. Some are homeless; some are financially affluent and well educated. Nevertheless, the common denominator is they are broken in one way or another. In his book *Rebuilding Your Broken World*, Gordon MacDonald said,

"Almost every one of us will encounter some issue that introduces us to brokenness at a far greater intensity that we ever thought possible...Broken worlds are a significant part of living; we must be vigilant enough to avoid the avoidable, but prepared and disciplined enough to persevere when facing the unexpected or the unavoidable."[1] Someone once said, "Into every life some rain must fall."

We all, at one time or another, experience some brokenness. The challenge is when you are broken you will fall into what John Bunyan called the "slough of despond." This is a state of despair and despondency, which causes you to quit. You become emotionally a wreck. And in this state, you limp your way through life. There are two ways in which we are broken:

1. Voluntarily...Here you yield to God's dealings in your life with a positive attitude
2. Involuntarily...Here things happen when you least expect it: sickness, death, accident. You respond negatively.

Why do broken experiences come? How do you respond? So many people are broken in the wrong places. I believe God desires to break our selfish

"Live Embracing Brokenness"

wills but not our spirits. For example, every parent has to be careful in disciplining their children that they do not crush their spirit as well as their will.

Some people respond to broken experiences: one, making excuses, self-justification; or two, the blame game – someone else's fault; or three, filling one's life with hectic activities while leaving it empty of God; and finally four, self-determination – I'll try harder on my own

So, what do I mean by brokenness? We must keep in mind what God's goal is in our brokenness. For example, see the words of John the Baptist in John 3:27-30, "...He must increase but I must decrease..." That is the goal of brokenness; denying oneself, becoming less so that Christ can become more. Therefore, brokenness is not:

1. Humility or repentance
2. Suffering or tears
3. Personal holiness or piety

However, brokenness is:

1. A heart allegiance to God
2. Total surrender to God
3. Crucified life unto God
4. Complete dependence upon God.

The broken person is one who no longer has the answer to their problems so they wait (sometimes in pain) upon God. Therefore, to be broken is to be subdued, humbled, crushed by grief, fragmented, and having self interrupted.

Make no mistake about it; God will use circumstances and situations in life to break us. I believe when God voluntarily breaks us, He does so in order to create a sense of more dependency upon Him and less dependency upon our natural strength. Broken people walk around with a limp as a tangible reminder because it reminds them of the experience of being broken. A few months ago, my doctor took a picture of my heart; what he saw was the scar from when I suffered my heart attack in September 1996. The scar is evidence that at a particular point in time there was some brokenness in my heart tissue.

The Scripture text tells the story of a man whom God broke and because of this brokenness, he suffered a limp when he walked. However, the story is much more than Jacob suffering a limp when he walked; it is about coming to a point in life were the only thing you want is God to bless you with His will for your life.

When the Old Testament speaks about God and His covenantal relationship with humankind it speaks of Him as the God of Abraham, Isaac, and Jacob. But He is also the God of Sarah, Rachel, and Rebekah.

The Bible is the story of how God enters into relationship with us. We are filled with selfish, self-centered, self-sufficient pride and arrogance. Yet, God comes to us in Jesus with the promise found in Luke 20:18, "Whoever fall on that stone will be broken, but on whomever it falls, it will grind him to powder." So, the question that I must answer is:

"Live Embracing Brokenness"

Have I fallen on the stone to be broken or is the stone falling upon me to be grinded to powder?

Jacob and Esau were twin brothers born to Isaac and Rebekah – (Genesis 25:19-26). The boys were different as night and day. Jacob was mild mannered, a mamma's boy; whereas Esau was wild and like to hunt. He was his father's favorite. One day, Esau came home from hunting and was hungry. He eventually gave up his birthright for some tasty stew (Genesis 25:22-34). Later, Rebekah concocted a plan to help her favored son Jacob deceive his father and take the blessing (Genesis 27:42-46). When Esau realizes that twice he had been deceived out of what was rightfully his, he planned to kill his brother the moment their father died. So, once Rebekah found out, she sent Jacob away to his uncle Laban. Over a 20-year period (Genesis 31:41), Laban deceived Jacob over and over. You reap what you sow!

Finally, Jacob desires to go back to his homeland; the place of his father. The problem is that Esau hears that Jacob was in the area and he's coming with 400 of his men! So Jacob is afraid. He devises a plan to split up his family and to send supplies out to Esau in hopes this would appease him (Genesis 22). Finally, Jacob is alone at the river Jabbok; Jabbok was a river east of the Jordan River. The meaning of the word Jabbok is to pour out or to empty (v 24) "…And a man wrestled with him until the breaking of the day." Who was this man who wrestled with Jacob? Hosea 12:2-4, identifies Him as an angel. As Jacob wrestled with this angelic being, he touched in the socket of his hip joint (v 25).

The angelic being told Jacob to let him go but Jacob refused. He insisted he wouldn't let go until he is blessed (v 26). So, the angelic being asked Jacob, "What is your name?" He said Jacob. Out of their discourse, Jacob has his named changed to Israel, prince with God or one who strives with God. No longer is his character that of a deceiver of supplanter (vv 27-28). A little later Jacob asked this angelic being his name. The angel finally blesses Jacob.

At the conclusion of this whole ordeal, Jacob calls the place "Penuel" which means "the face of God." As Jacob walked away, (v 31) says "...and the sun rose on him and limped on his hip."

The point of this story is simple. Whenever you reach the end of yourself and become broken, the battle scar of brokenness will always leave you with a limp. Just as Jacob wrestled with the angel, you and I will have to wrestle with our situations and trials until we are blessed through them. I believe your trials can make you stronger.

So, Andrae Crouch was very insightful when he wrote "Through it All", "I've had many tears and sorrows, I've had questions for tomorrow, there've been times I didn't know right from wrong; but in every situation God gave blessed consolation that my trials come to only make me strong. Through it all, through it all, I've learn to trust in Jesus, I've learned to trust in God. Through it all, through it all, I've learned to depend upon His word."[2]

I am reminded of the sacrifice of Jesus on the cross. He experienced brokenness: He was betrayed,

He was falsely accused, He was scourged, and finally, He was executed on a cross.

When He rose from the dead, He appeared to His disciples and showed them the nail prints in His wrist and the scars on His sides. So, Isaac Watts expressed this so well in his hymn, "At the Cross," "Alas! And did my Savior bleed? And did my sovereign die? Would He devote that sacred head for such a worm as I? At the cross, at the cross, where I first saw the light, and the burden of my heart rolled away – It was there by faith I received my sight, And now I am happy all the day!"[3]

Some of you, because of your trials, have wrestled with God in the midst of the situation. Because you have been bruised, you walk with a limp. Well, just keep on limping, because it is making a statement, which says...I am blessed! To live well is to recognize the benefits that can come through brokenness.

CHAPTER 7
"LIVE LIFE WITH JOY/LAUGHTER"

Psalm 16:11 (NKJV)

The problem with life is that it is daily. If life were one long weekend, it would be great. However, on Monday, you have to face your supervisor, coworker, or that problem at work. The daily grind of life will wear you down like a dull point on a pencil.

In the Fall of 2008, we were are all affected by the economic recession which has caused so much hardship to many, loss of jobs, loss of homes, and loss of confidence in the future.

There is certainly nothing to laugh about today because we are experiencing some hard times. This might come as a surprise to many of you but throughout much of church history, it was believed that fun and laughter was regarded as unspiritual

(especially the Puritans and some Holiness churches of the 19th century.)

In contrast to this view, take the perspective of Walt Disney, who believed life should be fun. With this mindset, he built Walt Disney World as a place where families could go away to have fun. Now you have Hershey Park, Six Flags among other theme parks. They have made millions of dollars doing one thing: allowing families to have fun. I believe that the best life is lived filled with fun and laughter. I want to give you permission to loosen-up and have some fun. Proverbs 17:22 says, "A merry heart does good like medicine, but a broken spirit dries the bones." In Zephaniah 3:17, the writer states, "The Lord your God in your midst, the mighty one, will save, He will rejoice over you with gladness, He will quiet you with His love, He will rejoice over you with singing."

A research article in *Psychology Today* entitled "Chronic Illness and Laughter," indicated that laughter has a positive effect on various ailments and diseases. Laughter releases endorphins, which helps to relieve pain in the body and brings a feeling of euphoria. When you laugh, you release hormones which research has shown reduces stress, strengthen the immune system, and make you feel more relaxed.[1]

Research has also shown that even a fake smile or false laughter has strong benefits. The Bible uses such words as rejoice, joy, laughter, pleasure, and happiness hundreds of time! Therefore, God is not against you having fun! In fact, Jesus was a frequent guest at dinner parties; see John 2:1-11, the wedding

"Live Life with Joy/Laughter"

at Cana of Galilee, and in Matthew 11:18-19, some called Jesus a wine bibber, a partygoer.

Psalm 16 is a song of David. Its basic message has to do with the hope of the faithful person and the triumph of the holy one, the Messiah. It is sub-captioned "A Michtam" which means relief from serious trouble. Other Psalms which are called Michtams, are Psalms 56-60. Psalm 16 is quoted by Peter in Acts 2:25-28. He is referring to Jesus Christ and the power of His resurrection.

I want to focus our attention on Psalm 16:11 …"Show me the path of life…In your presence…" Do you long for the presence of God in your life? I was inspired by a wonderful song written by the gospel artist, Byron Cage; "The presence of the Lord is here, the presence of the Lord is here, I can feel the presence of the Lord, and I'm going to get my blessing right now!"[2] Similarly, in Exodus 33:12-23, God promised His presence would go with Israel thus Moses' desire was to see the glory of God. The point to be made here is that there are two characteristics of the presence of God. First, the "fullness of joy", which means to leap or to dance. 1 Peter 1:8 speaks of "joy unspeakable and full of glory," and in Galatians 5:27, the fruit of the spirit is "joy."

Do you remember the occasion when King David danced before the Lord? In other words, this is the expression fullness of joy (II Samuel 6:12-14). Fullness of joy will make you get out of character… fullness of joy will make you praise as if you've lost your mind! Fullness of joy is an expression of thanks and appreciation for what God has done in Jesus Christ.

Second, "At your right hand are pleasures forever more." In other words, all the heart can desire, the sheer delight of living is found in our relationship with God. There are all sorts of pleasures:

- Sexual
- Relationships
- Food
- Watching a Broadway play

Psalm 1:2 "But his delight is in the law of the Lord, and in His law he meditates day and night" and Psalm 40:8 "I delight to do your will, O my God, and your law is within my heart" and Luke 12:32 "It is your father's good pleasure to give you the kingdom". The point to be made is simply this: So, the path of life is in the presence of God and in His presence are the fullness of joy and the abundance of pleasure. If you think about it, what I have shared will require us to change our minds about how we have been traditionally taught regarding God and our relationship with Him. **God wants us to have fun, to experience pleasure, to have joy, and most importantly, to experience true happiness**.

How then, do you live life with more joy and laughter? You must make a decision that you won't take life so serious all the time, stop being a workaholic, learn to balance your life and do something which is "fun".

- Vacation
- Leisure
- Go to a comedy club
- Don't be so serious all the time

The following humorous antidotes from *Church Bulletin Bloopers* were sent to me by a member of my church. I thought they were a riot and I hope you enjoy them as I did:

- "The Fasting & Prayer Conference includes meals."
- "Ladies, don't forget the rummage sale. It's a chance to get rid of those things not worth keeping around the house. Bring your husbands."
- "Remember in prayer the many who are sick of our community. Smile at someone who is hard to love. Say 'Hell' to someone who doesn't care much about you."
- "Don't let worry kill you off-let the Church help."
- "Miss Charlene Mason sang, 'I will not pass this way again,' giving obvious pleasure to the congregation."
- "Next Thursday there will be tryouts for the choir. They need all the help they can get."
- "At the evening service tonight, the sermon topic will be 'What Is Hell?' Come early and listen to our choir practice."
- "Potluck supper Sunday at 5:00 PM – prayer and medication to follow."

- "The ladies of the Church have cast off clothing of every kind. They may be seen in the basement on Friday afternoon."
- "This evening at 7 PM there will be a hymn singing in the park across from the Church. Bring a blanket and come prepared to sin."
- Low Self Esteem Support Group will meet Thursday at 7 PM. Please use the back door.
- "The eighth-graders will be presenting Shakespeare's Hamlet in the Church basement Friday at 7 PM. The congregation is invited to attend this tragedy."
- "The Associate Minister unveiled the church's new campaign slogan last Sunday: 'I Upped My Pledge – Up Yours.'"

Finally, in a cultural milieu that is preoccupied with pleasure and with the philosophy of hedonism, I believe Dr. John Piper is correct when he said, "God is most glorified in me when I am most satisfied in Him…"[3] If you desire to live well, then you must make time for fun.

CHAPTER 8
"LIVE BY NOT THINKING LIKE THE WORLD"
Ephesians 4:17-24; 1 John 2:15-17 (NKJV)

A few years ago, the United Negro College Fund did an advertising campaign that said, "A mind is a terrible thing to waste." I believe what you think means more than anything else in your life: more than what you earn, more than where you live, more than your social status, and more than what anyone else says or think about you. Furthermore, the longer I live the more I am convinced that there are only two types of people: those who stop to think and those who stop thinking! Proverbs 23:7 says, "For as he thinks in his heart so is he." What a person thinks greatly determines what they will become.

In January 1933, Dr. Carter G. Woodson, the father of Black History month, wrote in his seminal book *The Mis-Education of the Negro*, "When you control a man's thinking you do not have to worry about his actions. You do not have to tell him not to stand here or go yonder. He will find his proper place and stay in it. You do not need to send him to the back door. He will go without being told. In fact, if there is no back door, he will cut one for his special benefit."[1]

I believe that we are living in a "feeling" culture and not a "thinking" culture and as a result, Christians act no differently than their unsaved coworkers, neighbors, and family. I want to challenge you: don't allow the culture to dictate to you how you relate to God…your faith.

I also want to challenge you to cultivate a more biblical worldview, which will take a retraining of your mind and renewal of how you think about life. John Wooden once said, "It's what you learn after you know it all that counts." My friends, there are two types of minds:

1. The worldly mind that is grounded in the concerns of the contemporary culture.
2. The biblical mind that is grounded in the concerns of the kingdom of God.

The apostle Paul's letter to the church at Ephesus is addressed to a group of believers who are rich beyond measure in Jesus Christ, yet they were living as beggars because of the way they were thinking. Paul begins by describing in chapters 1-3, the believers' heavenly bank account: adoption, acceptance, redemption, forgiveness, wisdom, the seal of the Holy Spirit, the life of grace and not of bondage. He concludes in chapters 4-6, describing the believers walk and their warfare in Jesus Christ. The crucial point is the success of our wealth, walk, and warfare in Jesus Christ is depended upon our renewed thinking. Listen to this text in several different translations:

- "And so I insist—and God backs me up on this—that there be no going along with the crowd, the empty-headed, mindless crowd. They've refused for so long to deal with God that they've lost touch not only with God but with reality itself. They can't think straight anymore. Feeling no pain, they let themselves go in sexual obsession, addicted to every sort of perversion" (The Message Bible).[2]
- "With the Lord's authority I say this: Live no longer as the Gentiles do, for they are hopelessly confused. Their minds are full of darkness; they wander far from the life God gives because they have closed their minds and hardened their hearts against him. They have no sense of shame. They live for lustful pleasure and eagerly practice every kind of impurity" (The New Living Translation).[3]
- "So I'm telling you this, and I insist on it in the Lord: you shouldn't live your life like the Gentiles anymore. They base their lives on pointless thinking, and they are in the dark in their reasoning. They are disconnected from

God's life because of their ignorance and their closed hearts" (Common English Bible).[4]

Paul's point is this: You must make up in your own mind what type of mind will characterize your lifestyle:

1. The worldly mind–grounded in the concerns of the contemporary culture.
2. The biblical mind–grounded in the concerns of the kingdom of God.

Let me give you two illustrations that will make this point clearer:

- First, Martha Stewart, when she was released after being sentenced two years in prison for insider trading, was asked how she survived; she said, "it was all a matter of my thinking. I kept my mind focused upon the fact that this maybe where I am, but it is not where I ultimately will be." Currently, she is more popular than ever.
- Second, Michael Vick, when he was released after he was sentenced to prison for 18 months because of his involvement in a dog fighting enterprise, he lost everything. But he said it was his thinking about God, which sustained him. He was back in the NFL as the starting quarterback for the Philadelphia Eagles.

"Live by Not Thinking Like the World"

'In our text, Ephesians 3, the apostle Paul defines for us the way the worldly-minded person thinks:

1. (v. 17) " The futility of their minds" the Greek word *mataiotes* means emptiness, vanity, pointless. The idea here is there is a lack of content or substance. There is a lot of glitter but no gold. There is a lot of sizzle but no substance.
2. (v. 18-19) "Their understanding darkened, being alienated from the life of God." Because of their ignorance about the new life in Jesus. Because of their "harden heart…the Greek word porosis, means callous. The loss of feeling or sensation.
3. (vv. 20-24) The apostle Paul will give to us the process of how we go about changing the way we think. One, you must intentionally and daily practice renewing your mind. Approach it as if you were learning a new skill. Two, the way in which the apostle Paul approaches this is by using the idea of "putting on" and "putting off." The principle is consistent practice until it becomes second nature. Three, put off your former way of thinking…the old nature. And four, put on your new way of thinking… the renewed nature. The new nature is a work of the Holy Spirit.

Finally, if I am going to stop thinking like the world, I am going to need my mind to be renewed by the Holy Spirit! A mind is a terrible thing to waste. Why are you wasting your mind with:

- Jealously?
- Guilt?
- Shame?
- Greed?
- Sexual Immorality?
- Revenge?
- Low self-esteem?

Once again, if you are going to live well, you must cultivate a mindset, which consistently questions the way the culture thinks, and acts.

CHAPTER 9

"LIVE BY DEVELOPING AN ETERNAL PERSPECTIVE"

*Romans 12:1-2; Proverbs 23:7,
John 2:15-17 (NKJV)*

I think the fundamental point to be made about cultivating a biblical worldview is that it will take a conscious effort to retrain our minds; in other words, our thinking has to be renewed. Having been in pastoral leadership for over thirty years, it just seems to me, far too many Christians have been more influenced by the prevailing winds of the culture, so that, there is basically, little or no distinction between them and the non-Christian.

I believe that if you are going to live well, you must recognize that there is a temporary nature about life. Therefore, our focus needs to be upon more than just the temporary, but upon the transcendent. At some point in your life, you will inevitably ask the question: Is there life beyond death? I believe God has placed within each of us the spark of eternity. When I mention cultivating an eternal perspective, what exactly am I referring too? One, the entire process of renewing one's mind, which is aided by the Holy Spirit. We have to get in tune with the work of the Holy Spirit as He is working to transform our thinking. Two, the process of cultivating a biblical worldview or what I like to refer to as a "biblical mindset" is a conscious design. In other words, you must not only yield to the Holy Spirit, but you must choose a different way of thinking. Three, you must wrestle with the paradox about the nature of God; He is both transcendent and imminent. Here we are plunged into theology 101, God is omnipresent. The word transcendence means "above and beyond". Clearly, God the Father abides beyond our physical perspective. The word imminent means "here and now". Clearly, God the Son, Jesus, manifested a physical presence within our realm of perception.

Finally, you must critically evaluate all the nuances of secularism, which seeks to eradicate anything that can be considered sacred. I believe that one of the great dangers to living well is the ever-encroaching secularism of this postmodern culture. I concur with Dr. John MacArthur's comment, "A truly Christian worldview begins with the conviction that God Himself has spoken in Scripture…unless that axiom dominates our perspective on all of life, we cannot legitimately claim to have embraced a Christian worldview."[1]

"Live By Developing an Eternal Perspective"

There is a plethora of obstacles to living well and to developing an eternal perspective. In other words, any number of worldviews competes for our attention. Allow me to enumerate just a few:

1. Secularism. Essentially this means that ultimate reality is right here and now; thus, there is no such thing as transcendent reality. Hence, no God!
2. Postmodernism. There are no unifying narratives, which explain reality; there are no ethical absolutes; reality is essentially relative or contextual.
3. Materialism which means that all material matter such as cosmos is eternal and not created by a transcendent Deity.
4. Existentialism, which has as its mantra "existence precedes essence." You are the sum total of the choices you've made.
5. Humanism, which holds humankind as the supreme, without any need from God.

Once again, if you are going to live well, you must cultivate an eternal perspective. There are several passages of Scripture that press this crucial issue in the life of a Christian. Ecclesiastes 3:11 states, "He has made everything beautiful in its time. Also He has put eternity in their hearts,.." In other words, there is a sense within everyone that there must be another reality, which is greater than the present one. In Psalm 91:1-17, there is articulated beautifully the sense of the awesomeness of God in contrast with the frailty of human existence. I believe the apostle Paul is teaching this very principle in Philippians 3:20, "for our citizenship is in heaven, from which we also eagerly wait for the Savior, the Lord Jesus Christ." I don't believe he could have stated it any clearer than Romans 12:1-2, where he admonishes the Christians at Rome not to be conformed to the thinking of the surrounding culture but instead they must choose to be transformed or changed by renewing their minds. I believe this transformation occurs when we routinely meditate upon the Word of God.

I believe that cultivating an eternal perspective is beneficial for the following reasons:

- it gives you confidence in defending what you believe and why.
- it will protect you from being deceived by erroneous teachings.
- it is an aspect of "worshipping God with all our minds."
- it will help shape your thinking about such critical subjects as the nature of God, the nature of humankind, the sufficiency of the death of Christ regarding salvation, and the nature of one's ultimate destiny

Living well is not being independently wealthy and living a lavish lifestyle. No, living well means that one lives life with eternity in mind. To think and to live in this manner only betters one's faith and guards one from capitulating to the oppressive dictator called worldliness.

CHAPTER 10

"LIVE BY THE MOTTO: DON'T WORRY TALK TO GOD"

*Matthew 6:25-34, Proverbs, 23:7,
and 1 Peter 5:7 (NKJV)*

I believe there are too many Christians who gullibly follow the dictates of the general cultural ethics, who are like children in the nursery rhythm, the Pied Piper. Many believers maybe unconscious of this but it seem to me they are more comfortable operating within the cultural worldview than within the eternal one. This secular culture asserts a tremendous amount of influence upon the believer and non-believer alike. I now believe there is no real distinction between the way Christians and non-Christians act or think. As an example in contrast, when you travel to Lancaster, PA, you will come across a community of people call the Amish. It is clear that they are very different from the general culture.

I think that one of the consequences of the rejecting of an eternal worldview is the conundrum of worry. Basically, worry is an anxiousness or anticipation that something is going to happen negatively in the future while passing through the present! I believe that one can be cured of the malady of worry by talking to God. But, we are entrenched by worry; it is a universal human emotion. Perhaps the reason why we worry is because too many of life's realities are out of our control. We worry about what other people are saying about us; we worry about the way we look; we worry about the future; we worry about finances; we worry about our relationships, and we worry about being worried! I think you cannot worry yourself to life, but you sure can worry yourself to death. Dr. Charles Mayo, of the famed Mayo Clinic once said, "Worry affects the circulation of the heart, the glands, and the whole nervous system. I have never met a man or know a man who died because of overwork, but I have known lots who died because of worry."[1]

If worry is not good for us, why do we persist in doing it? In my opinion, I believe, it is because of a lack of faith. You often hear pastors tell people to "take your burdens to the Lord and leave them" but because of a lack of faith, we tend to quickly pick them up again. Also, it could be that we don't know the difference between worry and concern. A worried person sees the problem, but a concern person solves the problem! You must learn to redirect your tendency to worry about what may or may not happen in the future and focus on the present, here and now. If you want to live well, don't worry, talk to God! Instead of worry, try replacing it with prayer.

In Matthew 6:25-34, Jesus is teaching on the folly of worry. First, worry is worthless (v25). The word worry in the original language is *merimnao*, which means to divide into parts. Most of the time it is translated to "anxiety" or "cares" as in 1 Peter 5:7. Jesus' point is a simple one: your life is much more than the accumulation of material things, such as food and clothing. Yet, so many people do worry about those things. I compare this to a woman who faithfully workout on a treadmill, she may walk several miles and work up quite a sweat. But, in actuality, she hasn't gone anywhere. Therefore, worry will cause you to work up a sweat but you are not going anywhere.

Second, worry is unnecessary because of who our Heavenly Father is (vv26-30). Jesus tells his audience to look at the birds and beautiful lilies out in the fields. God manages to feed the birds and He dresses the lilies. Of how much more value are we? In other words, if God can manage to feed the birds and dress flowers, by implication He can do the same for you. This lack of faith in the ability of God to care for His children is at the heart of worry, as I alluded to above.

Third, worry is unreasonable because of the real power of faith (vv31-33). Jesus says you need not worry about your basic necessities of life because your Father already knows you have such needs.

Thus, by worrying you manifest a lack of faith. I believe the power of faith can move the hand of God, as seen in Hebrews 11:1,6 and Romans 10:17. The non-believer seeks after these material things such as eating, drinking, and clothing because they don't believe in the generosity of God.

Now, Jesus makes an observation, which will cure the problem of worry, "But seek ye first the Kingdom of God and His Righteousness and all these things will be added unto you." (v33). In other words, we need to redirect our priorities to align ourselves with the priorities of God. God's priority is the Kingdom and once you are aligned with His priorities), all of the things we have need of will be supplied. The Kingdom has to do with the reign of God. The question you must ask yourself is, does Jesus reign over your life? Are you a devoted follower of Jesus or just a fan?

Finally, worry is useless because it does not change a thing, back to my treadmill illustration above (vv34). The fundamental problem with worry is our preoccupation about the future. Those who worry are trying to live for something in which they are anticipating in the future. But Jesus is simply saying learn the art of living one day at a time. I think, Psalm 90:12 expresses this point very well, "So teach us to number our days that we may gain a heart of wisdom." (NKJV)

A man had to attend an important business meeting in a particular city…He had arrived at the airport and ran through several areas only to get to the gate…There was a man dressed in a uniform who

"Live By the Motto: Don't Worry Talk to God"

---

ask him why was he so worried and in such a rush? He said, I have an important business meeting in Washington, DC. The man was very adamant, but the man in the uniform was quite calm…How can you be so calm?...The man in the uniform told him, "That I am the pilot, and this plane ain't going anywhere until I say so." Is Jesus your captain? Is He piloting the ship of your life? If you can say, "Yes He Is" then why worry, just talk to God.

CHAPTER 11

"LESSONS LEARNED OVER A LIFETIME"

Ecclesiastes 12:13-14; Deuteronomy 30:15 (NKJV)

Some of the best advice I have ever received came from Grandma Mother LuPearl Davis, a godly woman, who passed in the fall of 2007. She use to say such things as:

"Live to the glory of God," or "treat people right," or "pay your tithes" and "prayer changes things!" She was always sharing her struggles as a single mom raising six children in the 1950s and 60s.

I've had the honor of talking to people who are at the end of life and they are reflecting upon their regrets and achievements. I have sure learned a lot in such settings. In fact, one of the greatest lessons I learned was "The problem with life is that it is daily. And you will never be successful in life until you learn what to do with the dailyness of the life you are given."

We have been dealing with the theme, "Living Well." Jesus said in John 6:63, "The flesh profits nothing. It is the spirit that gives life. The words I speak are spirit and they are life." And in John 10:10 He says, "The thief comes but to steal, kill, and to destroy, But I have come that you might have life, and that more abundantly." So, what we have discovered is that living well involves the following characteristics:

- Live life as a worship unto God
- Live life in the fear of the Lord
- Live life with purpose and passion
- Live life with satisfying relationships
- Live to forgive
- Life life embracing brokenness
- Live life with joy/laughter

King Solomon is a sad figure in the history of Israel. He was the son of David, the greatest king of Israel. He built a tremendous temple for the worship of God. God had given to him the throne, and he succeeded his father David. He was a wise and intellectually savvy man. His wisdom showed in the story of the two women who claimed to be the mother of a baby; in the act of sheer brilliance, he ordered that the baby be cut in half, knowing that the true mother would rather lose the child than see him killed. He had many concubines and wives, which ultimately was his downfall. He wrote most of the Proverbs. Thus, he was one of the wisest men of his day.

"Lessons Learned over a Lifetime"

Near the end of his life, Solomon wrote Ecclesiastes, which means "The Preacher." When you study Ecclesiastes, many are shocked that such a book is in the Bible! Why? In Ecclesiastes, Solomon is very negative, pessimistic, and sarcastic. Observe the following to see what I mean.

- Ecclesiastes 1:1-4; 10-17, Vanity of life, in other words, life is futile and meaningless
- Ecclesiastes 2:1-8, Vanity of pleasure, this too is meaningless.
- Ecclesiastes 3:1-8, Everything has its time, life must be lived with a certain sense of timing
- Ecclesiastes 9:9, Life is vanity, again as the above-mentioned, life is futile.

So, Solomon has seen and done it all, and now as an old man he is sharing his thoughts upon the meaning of life. Solomon is really struggling with the meaning of his existential existence and his basic conclusion is that life appears to have no real meaning or purpose at all!

When we study the book of Ecclesiastes, there are several lessons we can all learn from King Solomon as he shares with us "lessons learned over a lifetime," which will help us to live well.

- In the final analysis, human wisdom will prove to be empty and meaningless. This is not a knock of education but don't fool yourself; there are many educated fools! The focus ought to be upon the content of our character and what kind of person we are becoming? So many people today have allowed their education and their material prosperity to replace God.

- You must come to grips with the laws, which govern life. You will face suffering and challenges in this life. Be prepared for bad things to happen. Be prepared to be hurt, to be betrayed, and to be disappointed. Know this: The problem with life is that it is daily! Life happens.
- There is no lasting happiness in earthly goods and fleshly passions. Don't be defined by your accomplishment...you must have transcendent values. Enjoy your stuff but don't get too attached to them. Recognize the principle of diminishing returns. How long can you love that dress, car, and house?
- You must cultivate a sense of humility and gratefulness for the life you now live. Pride is just stupid! Solomon does recognize this fact; God has been good to him. Have you ever thought about what your life would be like if you were born in a different period of history? 1850s during slavery and 1920s during the depression?
- Finally, Solomon comes to his conclusion, (v.14) "For God will bring every work into judgment, including every secret thing, whether good or evil." In other words, you may choose to live life on your own terms, doing whatever you desire oblivious to the

ultimate reality God will one day hold you accountable for your choices.

The apostle Paul would say the same thing: "Be not deceived, God is not mocked whatever a man sows, that he will also reap" (Galatians 6:7). So, to live well one must live in dependence upon the presence of God. To live well is to live in the fear of God, which is our reverence toward God. The best kind of life is one lived doing what he tells you to do. The best kind of life is one lived in the light of eternity. In other words, in the consciousness that Jesus is coming back one day, so how ought I to live?

You can't live the best kind of life in your own strength but you will need Jesus Christ to show you the way. You see, it was Jesus who said, "I am the way, the truth and the life." And 1 Peter 2:21 says, "For to this you were called, because Christ also suffered for us, leaving us an example, that you should follow His steps." Jesus taught us how to live well is now calling us to follow his example.

Endnotes

Preface

1. Viktor E. Frankl, *Man's Search For Meaning*. (Boston, MA; Beacon Press, 2006), p. 99
2. Rick Warren, *Purpose Driven Life*. (Grand Rapids, MI; Zondervan, 2002), pp 27-29
3. Source unknown regarding this quote.
4. Tony Evans, *The Battle Is the Lord's*. (Chicago, IL; Moody Press, 1998), pp 19-20
5. Warren, pp 42-47
6. Edward Mote, *The Solid Rock*. (Public Domain, 1834)

Chapter 1

1. Judson Cornell, *Let Us Worship*. (Plainfield, NJ; Bridge Pub., 1983), p. 97

Chapter 2

1. W.E. Vines, *Expository Dictionary of New Testament Words*. (McLean, VA; MacDonald Publishing Company), p424

Chapter 3

1. Myles Monroe, *The Pursuit of Purpose*. (Shippensburg, PA; Destiny Image, 1992), preface.
2. Ibid, Warren, p 17
3. Ibid, purposes themes 1-5, covers entire book...pp 63, 117, 171, 227, 281
4. J.B. Phillips, *The New Testament In Modern English*. (New York; MacMillan Company, 1959), p 341

Chapter 4

1. Theme from "Cheers" Sitcom seen during the 1980's. "Where Everybody Knows Your Name", Gary Portnoy and Judy Hert Angelo
2. Jerry and Mary White, *Friends and Friendship*. (Colorado Springs, CO; NavPress, 1983), p 12
3. Larry Crabb, *Connecting*. (Nashville, TN; Word Publishing, 1997), p 1

Chapter 5

1. Gary Thomas, *The Forgiveness Factor.* (Christianity Today, Vol. 44, no. 1-Jan 10, 2000), p38
2. R.T. Kendall, *Total Forgiveness*. (Lake Mary, FL; Charisma House, 2002) XXXII
3. Ibid., p 4
4. Ibid., p 21

Chapter 6

1. Gordon MacDonald, *Rebuilding Your Broken World*. (Nashville, TN; Thomas Nelson, 1988), Jacket Cover
2. Andre Crouch, "Through It All" (Public Domain, 1674 – 1748)
3. Isaac Watts, "At the Cross"

Chapter 7

[1] Psychology Today, August 25, 2009
[2] Byron Cage, "The Presence of The Lord Is Here", Lyrics, Kurt Carr, 2003
[3] John Piper, *Desiring God*. (Multnomah Books, Sisters, OR, 1996) p 95

Chapter 8

[1] Carter G. Woodson, *The Mis-Education of the Negro*. (Trenton, NJ; Africa World Press, 1990), preface.
[2] *The Message Bible*, Eugene H. Peterson, (Colorado Springs, CO; NavPress, 2002) p.2131
[3] *New Living Translation*, (2nd Edition, Tyndale House; Carol Stream, IL, 2007) p. 954
[4] *Common English Bible*, (Common English Bible; Nashville, TN, 2011) p. 205

Chapter 9

[1] John MacArthur, *Think Biblically,* (Crossway Books; Wheaton, IL, 2003) p.21

Chapter 10

[1] Fredrich A. William, *Aphorism of Dr. Charles H. Mayo and Dr. William J. Mayo*. (2008)

www.ingramcontent.com/pod-product-compliance
Ingram Content Group UK Ltd.
Pitfield, Milton Keynes, MK11 3LW, UK
UKHW041944230426
12048UKWH00008B/118